Extracts from leg
reproduced under

Other documents
domain and are used for educational purposes under fair dealing rules.

The use of any quotes or extracts does not imply any form of endorsement of the think1265 campaign, or our aims, by the authors or organisations quoted.

Iconography via noun project, used under licence.

Cover photo: Ron Lach (Pexels.com, copyright free)



ISBN: 978-10681-92807

Published by think1265.org

Printed by Three Creative Company Limited.

# Contents

# Introduction

Teachers' workload in Northern Ireland is managed by a complex set of contractual arrangements. It can therefore be difficult for teachers to know what their rights and entitlements are about when, where, and for how long, they are expected to work as part of their paid contract.

This complexity can also make it difficult for school leaders and governors to ensure that they are managing their staff workload within the terms and conditions negotiated and agreed by the Teachers' Negotiating Committee.

This Wee Little Book sets out to provide a quick reference document showing how each element of the working life of a teacher fits into the contractual landscape in which they work.

We hope it helps all stakeholders create the healthy, productive and sustainable work-life balance that educators need to effectively deliver the top-class education our young people deserve.

Brian and Helen. July 2025

# How to use this book

This book explains the rules about teacher workload in a simple way, so that a user can clearly see what should be happening in particular circumstances.

Since very few of these provisions have been tested in an employment tribunal, we use a star rating to indicate how reliable we believe our interpretation to be.

★★★ - Clear and unambiguous

★★ - Mostly clear and widely agreed

★ - Subject to ongoing debate

The superscript number(s) at the end of each of our statements links to the reference document(s) supporting our text, which are found on page 54-72.

*E.g. "Teachers must wear tweed [1, 3] ★★"*

*This statement is supported by reference 1 & 3 and is mostly clear and widely agreed.*

QR codes take the reader to supplementary material which may be useful.

**Important**: think1265 **are not** a trade union.

Readers should seek advice before taking any action which might breach their contractual obligations.

# Sources

We have based the information in this book on the teachers' contract ("The Jordanstown Agreement"), relevant TNC documents which interpret this contract, related legislation, and clarification we have received about various issues from official bodies.

Some issues are clear, but where there is debate we have tried to present relevant information about the various arguments to help users consider how an issue should be addressed where they work.

# About think1265

The think1265 teacher workload campaign was set up in April 2024 by two fulltime teachers. Our sole aim is to facilitate the implementation of existing workload agreements in all schools in NI by ensuring that all staff – teachers and leaders – are aware of what these agreements mean in their working lives.

These agreements exist because of the NITC, who work to improve the conditions of teachers in this country. All of us owe them our continued thanks.

Resolving workload issues in our schools can feel impossible. This book is dedicated to the teachers who make the impossible possible, twenty-one thousand times every day.

# Importance of union support

Among many other things, teaching Trade Unions (TUs) support educators with career issues. We **strongly** encourage you to join one.

There are four main teaching TUs in Northern Ireland: NASUWT; INTO, UTU, and NEU, serving teachers and school leaders. In addition to these there are NAHT and ASCL, who specialise in supporting school leaders.

1265

# What is Directed Time?

Directed Time (DT) is the time spent by a teacher on any activity the Principal has determined they shall undertake as part of their professional duties.[1] ★★★ Simply put, DT is a teacher's working hours.

All the time a teacher **must** be present on school premises is **automatically** DT.[1] ★★★

*Misconception – "Directed Time" is often used to describe the time teachers spend in school after students have left, but this is incorrect.* *(see page 16)*

A teacher cannot be directed by a **Principal**, a Principal's **representative**, or by a school **policy**, to work on these professional duties for **more than 1265 hours** (*pro rata*) in any one year.[4] ★★★

A teacher **cannot** be directed to work **on more than 195 days** in any one year.[3] ★★★

No more than **190** of these days can involve **teaching students**.[3] ★★★

A teacher's year starts on the 31st July, and a teachers' week starts on a Sunday.[5] ★★★

If a task is reasonably expected of a teacher by their Principal, then it **must** come out of the 1265 hours of DT.[6] ★★★

Time which a teacher chooses to spend off school premises engaged in the **preparing and marking of *lessons*** is **not** DT and does not come from the 1265 hours of directed time. [4] ★★★

Since this work is **not** part of DT it is **unpaid**.

The amount of unpaid time a teacher decides to spend in planning and marking lessons off the school premises is a **matter of professional judgement** for that teacher. They **cannot be directed** to do this work.[7] ★★★

Except for the preparing and marking of lessons mentioned above, **all** other professional duties **must** be included in the 1265 hours of DT.[6] ★★★

A teacher's workload should be such that they can normally complete all their professional duties within their **contractual hours.** [45] ★★★

Extra-curricular activities a teacher **volunteers** to do **are not** part of Directed Time. If a teacher is **directed** to do these then they become part of DT and come out of the 1265 hours / 195 days. [10] ★★★ (see p22)

Teachers' time is the most expensive use of taxpayers' money in education, and the mechanism to ensure that Principals direct that resource to where it is most impactful is called the "Directed Time budget".

# The Directed Time budget

It has been the **Principal's responsibility** to decide how a given teacher will spend their 1265 hours / 195 days each year since 1987. [11,28] ★★★

The mechanism to do this is called the Directed Time budget (DTB). It is a **formal document**, and it should be distributed to teachers **prior to the start** of the teaching year. [12] ★★★

Principals should try to **reach agreement** with each teacher about the tasks that teacher will perform, and the time they will spend on each task. [12] ★★★

DTBs should be **individualised**, considering the responsibilities of each teacher.[12] ★★★.

Think of a DTB as the "to do" list the Principal wants a particular teacher to do in that academic year.

If a DTB is poorly planned a teacher can **run out of hours** for certain tasks for that year. [13] ★★.

If this happens then that teacher is **not** contractually obliged to complete these tasks unless (a) more time is provided for them by removing other tasks; (b) they get overtime or TOIL for this work, or (c) they are paid separately for it on an additional contract.

The reason this rarely happens is because teachers rarely track the hours they spend on various tasks.

The current gold standard for DTBs are the templates provided by the Education Authority, which can be found here:

Marking and moderation of coursework and controlled assessment, internal examinations, and other batch marking may need added to these templates. See pages 28 & 30-31.

## The 3 T's of DTBs

Are **all** necessary **TASKS** for that teacher clear and included on the DTB? Is there **sufficient TIME** allocated for each task to be completed? Is there a **clear TIMESLOT** in the weekly, termly or annual timetable when this work will happen?

Another useful acronym is "**CRAM**". Tasks should be **C**lear, with **R**easonable time allocated. They should also be **A**greed and **Monitorable**.

We have developed a simple tool on our website to highlight issues with a DTB:

Principals should **avoid** large blocks of "Contingency Time" or "Professional Duties," as these are essentially non-directed.

Since teachers rarely tally their hours, these blocks never "run out", thus driving excessive workload. EA recommends about 6 hours for contingency time for emergencies in their DTB templates.

# The School Day – before school

In many schools some teachers arrive **before** the official start time of the school day.

If a teacher uses this time to **prepare or mark lessons**, this will probably be part of the unpaid PPA they **choose to do** themselves. [7] ★★

If a teacher carries out **other professional duties** during this time, whether this time is counted as part of their DT depends on their school's working hours.

Some teachers are required to be in school for the full 32.4 hours per week.[14] Such teachers have no "spare" hours from their 1265, and they **cannot** be **directed** or **expected** to carry out **professional duties** before the school day starts. [10] ★★★

If working hours are less than 32.4 hours per week, allowing **flexibility** about when and where DT is carried out, professional duties before school starts **can count** as part of that teacher's 1265 hours.

Some teachers have formal supervision duties before school starts, and these **must be fully accounted for** in their DTB. [15] ★★★

Additionally, setting up (and derigging) a classroom is **not** part of PPA, and must be accounted for in a teacher's Directed Time. [30] ★★★

# The School Day – Registration

**Registration** is part of DT and must be included in a teacher's DTB. [16] ★★★

Simply taking a registration and ensuring good order is considered **supervision**. This "non-contact" time **is not** part of the weekly teaching hours. [15] ★★

If a teacher is required to deliver learning or carry out pastoral work with a student or group of students during registration, this is considered **teaching time**. This time **is** part of weekly teaching hours. [16] ★★★

# Assembly

Attendance at an assembly is DT and must be accounted for in the DTB. Just **attending** an assembly is considered **supervision** and is **not** part of a teacher's teaching time. [17] ★★★

**Leading** or **actively participating** in an assembly is considered "contact" and **must be** accounted for in that teacher's weekly teaching hours. [17] ★★ (p17)

*We have made the above "amber" because there could be argument about the meaning of "contact" in an assembly. We consider actively participating (i.e. facilitating a learning experience) as "teaching time", to be treated the same as "leading".*

# School Day – Teaching Time

Teaching time is the easiest element of workload to understand. For most teachers, teaching time can be calculated from a timetable or from school operating times.

However, teaching time also includes other activities which are harder to track, such as pastoral work, revision classes, or leading an assembly.

There are several restrictions on teaching time which must be observed:

A full-time teacher cannot be asked to teach on more than **190** days per year. [3]★★★

A post-primary teacher cannot be directed to teach more than **23.5 hours** per week, while in a primary or special school this rises to **25 hours.**[20] ★★★

NB: this must be calculated on a **weekly basis,** so periodic directions **do not** take a teacher over this limit *for that week*. If this happens a teacher should inform their line manager as soon as possible.

Having a teacher **available** for cover is considered teaching time, **even if that cover session is not used** on a given week. [18,20]★★★

# School Day – Cover

**Cover** for absent colleagues **is part** of Directed Time, and time **must** be allocated for this on a teacher's DTB for them to join the cover rota. [37,6]★★★

Cover **is not** supervision and **is part** of a teacher's "teaching time."[18,6]★★★

Schools should have an easily accessible **cover policy**, regularly monitored by the Principal in consultation with recognised Trade Union reps, ensuring **fair and equitable distribution** of cover duties among teaching staff. [38 39 43]★★★

Teachers **cannot** be **directed** to cover an unplanned absence **after** the **second day** of absence (other than for nursery, P1 or P2 classes.) [40]★★★

Teachers **cannot** cover agreed planned absences **at all** if they are to **exceed 2 days absence** (other than for nursery, P1 or P2 classes.) [40]★★★

**NQTs** on long-term contracts should only undertake cover in **exceptional** circumstances. [41]★★★

Teachers **cannot** be directed to cover classes **at all** in schools with average enrolment **of 222 or fewer** students. [40]★★★

If a **TA holder** is directed to **produce work** for cover, this is **DT** and **must** be on their DTB. [34]★★★

# School Day – Break and Lunch

Most schools have a firmly established **breaktime** for pupils, but this is **not** a formal break for teachers. For teachers, breaktime is Directed Time, and **must** appear on their Directed Time Budget. [15] ★★★

Most teachers will be a part of a **rota** covering breaktime supervision. On days where a teacher is **not required** for breaktime supervision it is **still** Directed Time, **must** be on their DTB, and **must** come out of their 1265 hours.[15] ★★★

In schools where teachers are used for break supervision, school leaders should consider H&S and Equality legislation, along with basic staff dignity, ensuring staff can access a toilet during the school day.

Teachers must have an **uninterrupted break** of at least 30 minutes between 12pm and 2.30pm (nursery classes), or between 12pm and 2pm (other settings). [26] ★★★ This break is **unpaid** [26,30] ★★★ and can be taken **on or off-site**.

A teacher **cannot** be directed to work during this break, unless paid through a separate lunchtime supervisor contract. [15] ★★★

# School Day – Afterschool DT

The 1987 Jordanstown Agreement introduced the concept of Directed Time, placing limits on teachers' working hours equating to approximately 32.4 hours per week.

Since a typical school week (minus lunch) is 30 hours per week, many staff were "directed" to stay in school to work the additional 2.4 hours. This practice became synonymous with DT itself.

In fact, the contract states that teachers can be directed to work *"at such times and **such places** as may reasonably be specified by the Principal"* [4] ★★★ "Such places" **can** include at home.

In practice, though, many schools will have one or more days a week where DT events are scheduled after school. These events **must** be on the annual calendar, which **must** be provided before the start of the academic year. [24] ★★★

If a school finishes at 3.30pm and afternoon DT starts at 3.45pm, the 15 minutes between is known as "**trapped time**" (see also pp 35) and **must** be included in DT. [29] ★★★

**Twilights** are another form of afterschool Directed Time and are dealt with on page 36.

## School Day – Other Duties

During a school year there are other duties which teachers can be directed to do. These are **all** considered Directed Time and **must** be accounted for in that teacher's DTB. [1,6] ★★★

Whether these duties are considered "contact" (i.e. teaching time) depends on their nature. [15] ★★

For example, supervising a corridor as students leave, or taking part in bus duty, **is** Directed Time but **is not** teaching time. This is because no active teaching is required on these occasions. [15] ★★★

Supervising after-school detention **is** Directed Time but **is not** teaching time as the teacher merely supervises students to complete work and maintain order. [15] ★★★

However, if a teacher is **directed** to run an after-school session where active learning is taking place, then this session **is both** Directed Time **and** teaching time. [1,6,15] ★★★ Running a session **voluntarily** is **not DT** or **teaching time.**[10]★★★ (See p22 for more information.)

The importance of tracking teaching and non-teaching Directed Time is explained on page 18.

# Teaching and Non-Teaching DT

There is a strict limit on the amount of "contact" time (i.e. teaching time) that teachers in Northern Ireland can be asked to do each week.

Teachers in the primary and special sectors cannot be required to teach more than **25 hours in any week.** [21] ★★★

Teachers in the post-primary sector cannot be required to teach more than **23.5 hours in any week.** [21] ★★★

Teacher workload agreements are focused on enhancing teaching and learning, promoting a reasonable work/life balance, and ensuring that the spirit and law of Health and Safety legislation is followed. [22] ★★★

H&S legislation places responsibility on employees too[23] ★★★, so teachers must ensure that their contact time each week does not exceed the limits above, informing their line managers if it does.

NB: If a teacher is to be available for **cover** each week, this time **is included** in teaching time [27] ★★★ and **must** be on their DTB – even if that time is **not used** for cover on a given week.

# Meetings and Training

Meetings and training sessions **are part** of Directed Time, **must** be fully accounted for in Directed Time budgets, and **must** come out of a teacher's 1265 *pro rata* annual hours. [24] ★★★

A school **must provide** a schedule of **all planned** meetings in advance of the start of the academic year. [24] ★★★ (See also p40.)

While this schedule can be changed, this should only be through **consultation** and **agreement** with staff and recognised Trade Unions. [9] ★★

If **new meetings** are introduced during the year time should be **freed** from other tasks to facilitate these new meetings. [6] ★★★

Teachers' time costs money, so school leaders should ensure that meetings are good value for that money. This calculator estimates the "on costs" for meetings.

If students leave at 3.30pm and a meeting starts at 3.45pm, the 15 minutes in between is **trapped time** and is part of teachers' Directed Time. [29] ★★★

# Professional Communications

The Jordanstown Agreement gives a list of the Professional Responsibilities of teachers, and at least 10 require communication to fulfil. [32] ★★★

Professional communications is **work**, and time to do this work **must** be included in a teacher's DTB and **accounted for** in their 1265 hours. [6] ★★★

Time for digital communications **must** also be accounted for in a teacher's DTB, including email, SIMS, Google Classroom, Dojo, *etc*.

*NB: DE offers eye test support for staff who regularly use VDUs for more than 1 hour per day.* [33] ★★

Time for phone calls **must** also be accounted for in a teacher's DTB.

Teachers with **pastoral** responsibilities may require more communication time to carry out their roles properly, and time should be provided for them to do so. [6,34] ★★★

Teachers should track hours spent on these tasks in their planner. This calculator 👉 helps estimate the time they need throughout the year.

## Communication with Parents

Communication with parents is **work**, and time to do this **must** come out of a teacher's Directed Time budget. [6] ★★★

This includes communications via **digital learning platforms,** or by **face-to-face** meetings. Time to prepare – such as gathering information – and time to complete post-communication admin (such as contact logs) must also be included. [6] ★★★

Teachers with **pastoral**, **disciplinary** and **safeguarding** functions often need more time to communicate with parents, and that **must** also be accounted for. [34] ★★★

Some schools facilitate these functions by providing these teachers with **cover** to facilitate this work, which is "time-budget neutral". Other schools utilise administrative staff to help with communications, which eases teacher workload. Teachers should find out if such help exists, and use it if it does.

Schools **must** communicate **operational hours** to parents, so they know that staff are **not expected** to respond outside of school hours. [35] ★★★

Teachers should **never** use their personal devices, numbers or emails to communicate with parents.

# Extracurricular activities

TNC 2024/2 section 5.2 says *"... schools have always been dependent on a commitment from Teachers beyond the legal minimum requirement...*[10]

Unlike the "Zombie clause" (p26) this phrase **does not** refer to professional duties. Instead, it refers to **extracurricular activities**, such as games, drama, music, PTA events, and school trips *etc.*[10]★★★

It is **entirely** up to a teacher how much time – if any – they want to spend on these activities. [10]★★★

If a teacher **volunteers** to do an extracurricular activity, **it does not count** as Directed Time. [10]★★★

If a teacher is **directed** to do an extracurricular activity, then **it is** Directed Time. [10]★★★

Such directions **count** toward the 195 annual days, even if brief, or during weekends / holidays. [10]★★★

There is no obligation for schools to compensate staff for **voluntary** extracurricular work, but many do.

Schools **must** ensure that teachers who volunteer for such activities have a **work/life** balance.[6, 8] ★★★

If a teacher feels they are treated unfairly because they don't do extra-curricular activities they should contact their union to discuss the matter.

### Trips and overnight stays

While teachers **can** be directed to take students on trips out of school, they **cannot** be directed to take students on trips involving **overnight stays.** [44] ★★★

If a teacher chooses to do this on a **voluntary** basis, they **can** negotiate with the Principal to have DT hours allocated to this on a goodwill basis. Although there is no official formula for calculating such time, it **should** include sufficient school time for the organisation of such visits.[44] ★★★

Teachers involved in time-hungry activities such as plays could discuss their time requirements with their Principal, but time negotiation for these events is not specified in the TNCs. Principals may provide some time for these activities on a goodwill basis.

Schools **must** ensure that teachers involved in such work have a **healthy work/life balance.** [6, 8] ★★★

Teachers also have the right to **reasonable workloads** and **a fair distribution** of work within the school. This should be considered when teachers are involved in extra-curricular activities. [45] ★★★

Taking students off school premises **carries risks** which must be fully managed. It involves additional workload and responsibilities which should be discussed when agreeing the contents of a DTB.

## Planning and preparing lessons

Quality PPA is essential to produce quality lessons, however PPA time was not formally included in Directed Time budgets until 2020. [48] ★★★

Since then, teachers **must** receive a **minimum** of **10%** of their DT hours as ringfenced PPA. [46] ★★★

PPA time is to **raise** standards and improve teachers' **work/life balance**. [46] ★★★ Post-primary teachers get part of this as **non-contact** periods (teachers don't get "free" periods), while other settings have this time **outside** of the pupils' day or through internal cover.

PPA can be **individual** or **collaborative**, and leaders must ensure that it **is not** eroded by other demands. [49] ★★★

The practice of teachers having to produce planners several weeks in advance to a certain format for internal manager appraisal is contentious. It is a **direction**, so sufficient time should be given for this task in a teachers' DTB. [6] ★★★ Using the 10% PPA time to complete such planners **erodes** that time, [49] ★★ and teachers **cannot** be directed to do this outside of their DT hours. [10] ★★★

The use of teachers' time to prepare medium / long-term planners is under scrutiny by Management side as a potential driver of excessive workload. [50] ★★★

Principals can direct staff to do any reasonable task, including planner preparation, but time **must** be provided to teachers to do this work.

Large-scale marking tasks such as exams, controlled assessments, *etc.* will **erode** PPA time, so **separate time** should be provided for this work.

Similarly, PPA time is for **short-term** teaching and learning for a teacher's classes. Longer-term planning needs separate time provided. [7] ★★★

As with all DT, PPA can happen at a place of the Principal's choosing. [1] ★★★ This is a matter of negotiation with the Principal and teacher reps.

**TA holders** on reduced contact hours **must still** receive 10% PPA time in their DTB. [47] ★★★

Unlike in England, there is no contractual provision that PPA time must be in chunks of 30 mins or more. However, blocks less than this will be less effective.

All teachers should have a suitable space to carry out their PPA without distraction.

PPA time is important, so teachers should jealously protect this time and raise issues with their line managers if it is being eroded by other demands.

# PPA outside of contracted hours

Teachers' annual contracted hours are 1265 hours over 195 days, *"exclusive of time spent off premises in preparing and marking lessons..."* [4] ★★★

We call this the "Zombie clause", as regardless of how many agreements attempt to limit teachers' additional work at home, it simply won't die.

Many workload agreements have contextualised and rationalised this clause, so what does it currently mean for teachers in 2025-26?

Let's break it down:

Preparing and marking **lessons** is one of the **professional duties** of teachers. [32(section 1.1, 1.3)] ★★★

If teachers **choose** to do this type of **PPA** for **lessons** outside of their contracted hours, this time is **not** part of their 1265 hours of Directed Time. [4] ★★★

The **amount of time** a teacher spends doing this is **up to** that teacher. [7] ★★★

If a teacher is **directed** to do PPA at home, then this time **must** come from that teacher's Directed Time budget as it has become a direction. [1,6] ★★★

All sides on the TNC agree that the practice of teachers doing PPA outside of normal teaching hours is **not considered satisfactory.** [46] ★★★

The "Zombie clause" does not refer to **any other** professional duty of teachers except preparing and marking lessons. **All** other professional duties **must** take place in Directed Time. [6] ★★★

The *"commitment from teachers beyond the legal minimum requirement...",* mentioned in workload agreements refers to **voluntary** activities (like sports or clubs), and **not** to carrying out professional duties in a teacher's free time. [10,6] ★★★

PPA at home **must comply** with H&S and Working Time law, and employers should take **all** reasonable steps to ensure the health and safety of their teachers is **protected** if doing this work. [8,51] ★★

Teachers have a **right** to **fair** and **reasonable** workloads, which can normally be carried out **within** contractual hours. [45] ★★★ If this isn't the case a teacher can **individually** or **collectively** raise this issue using this agreed mechanism. [36] ★★★

In summary: If a teacher **occasionally** needs to do **some PPA** outside of school hours, then that's probably fine. But if they are so busy in work that they end up doing **lots of PPA** on a **regular basis** then something might be going wrong, and they should talk to their line manager. If they regularly must do work **other than PPA** in their own time, then something is **definitely wrong** in their DTB, and they should talk to their manager or union rep.

# Periodic tasks – marking

Marking and assessment is a **professional duty** and constitutes **Directed Time.**[1,6] ★★★ The only type of marking which is not **automatically** DT is the marking of **lessons** (including homework) which a teacher **chooses** to **set** themselves. (See p26 & 27)

**All** the time a teacher needs to do the marking and assessment required of them by their managers **must** be provided in their DTB.[6] ★★★

Principals should determine how much time individual teachers need for marking **through consultation** when seeking to agree that teacher's DTB.[12] ★★★ This calculator 👉 can help a teacher identify how much marking time they will need.

Teachers can also be directed to carry out marking by a **school policy** that they are directed to follow. E.g. if a school has a homework policy, time to carry out this marking **must** be provided for in the DTB.

Marking time **must** include **all** the time needed from setting the work to uploading results.[6] ★★★

# The importance of policies

Policies tend to accrete over time, but school leaders should be aware that if a policy is still **active**, and if teachers are **meant to follow that policy,** then that policy is a **direction**, and **time** to implement it **must** come from a teacher's **DTB.** [6] ★★★

**Regularly reviewing policies** and procedures in consultation with Trade Unions, allows school leaders to manage workload at a granular level.

For example, **marking policies** often detail the level and quality of written feedback required when marking work. However, **the time** teachers require to reasonably carry out this marking **must** be provided in their DTB, making it a time-expensive policy.

A Principal is free to direct teachers to do any reasonable duty, but they must **pay** for that work out of teachers' available hours. Outdated policies can therefore **passively drain** this available teacher time from a Principal's resource pool – the time budget equivalent of that forgotten Netflix subscription.

Similarly, a teacher who does not have **sufficient identified time** to discharge a particular policy in their DTB would have a **strong defence** should a **dispute** arise about how well they have carried out that policy during the year.

## Coursework and Controlled Assessment

There is debate about how Coursework (CW) and Controlled Assessment (CA) marking fits into Directed Time. Let's break it down.

Marking CW/CA is a **professional duty**, described in point 6 of the list of teachers' duties. [32] ★★★

In some subjects students do small bits of CW during lessons, this can sometimes be marked as part of **normal 10% PPA** time. However, it **must not erode** PPA time to the detriment of other PPA.[49] ★★

While this might be possible on occasion for simple courses, the demands of L3 courses could erode all of this PPA time. Therefore, **dedicated time should** be provided for this work. [6] ★★★

Many schools provide teachers with time to do CW/CA work by providing cover or by collapsing timetables during busy times. This is "time budget neutral" but should ensure that **sufficient** time is given for each teacher's specific needs. [9,12,] ★★★

Time for CW/CA functions **must** include **all** the administrative tasks necessary, from setting up materials through to submitting results to the awarding body. [6] ★★★

It can be argued that some CW/CA marking could fall under the "Zombie clause", but this is **not** informal "marking of lessons" that a teacher chooses to do; rather it is formal marking for external bodies.

Teachers of CW/CA subjects **must** mark the work – it **is not** a matter of their professional judgement. [7]★★★ It is reasonable, therefore, to consider marking CW/CA as a **direction.** [6]★★★

Additionally, failing to mark coursework could have serious consequences for a teacher, but if no time is given from that teacher's contracted hours for this they could have a **strong defence** in a dispute.

Teachers also have a right to **fair** and **reasonable** workloads, normally **completed** in **contractual hours.** [45]★★★ If some teachers must mark CW/CA at home while other teachers don't, this would breach the TNC agreements about the fair and reasonable distribution of workload.

At the very least, employers should ensure that they are monitoring the amount of additional time their staff are working on these tasks, in order to ensure fair and open distribution of workload. [8,51] ★★

While marking of CW/CA is complex, there are important reasons to ensure that teachers have the time they need to do this job. How awarding bodies create these demands is also part of the current workload review, so CW/CA may change in 2025-26.

# Teaching Allowance Holders

Classroom teachers in Northern Ireland can be promoted within their school by applying for posts which carry "Teaching Allowances" (TAs).

These positions carry **leadership** and **school development** responsibilities; typically involve work that is **not** required of all classroom teachers, and which will have a wider impact within the school than everyday classroom teaching. [19] ★★★

These teachers are paid for this additional responsibility by receiving TA payments, on a 5-point scale, on top of their normal salary.

Teachers with Teaching Allowances **must receive sufficient time** to discharge their responsibilities from their 1265 hours of **Directed Time.** [34] ★★★

They must also receive a **schedule** of **meetings**, including all meetings pertaining to their role, **before** the start of the academic year. [24] ★★★

There is a misconception that Teaching Allowance work is **in addition to** a regular teacher's work and must be carried out in that **teacher's own time**. This is false. [34] ★★★

TA holders **cannot** be expected to do TA work outside of contracted Directed Time. If this happens they should talk to their manager and their union rep.

We have designed a calculator which can be used to break down the time a TA holder might need to discharge their role. 👉 This is a rough tool but helps to give a ballpark figure about how much time might be required at different times of the year.

Time for TA holders is normally granted by the **removal** of **teaching time**.

Many schools support TA holders by providing **cover** or **collapsed timetable** during times of the year when TA holders are particularly busy, which is "time budget" neutral.

Care should be taken with **pastoral** roles, such as Year Heads. The demands of these roles often increase because of events, so these staff should ask for more time when needed.

If a TA holder is provided with insufficient time to do their job, and if they monitor the time they spend on it during the year, they are at risk of running out of hours – something which Principals are warned about when designing DTBs. [13] ★★★ Therefore it is essential that teachers and Principals are realistic when determining the time demands of a particular TA role. [12] ★★★

# Equity, equality and fairness

Teachers in Northern Ireland have the right to workloads which are managed in an "open, fair and equitable way". [45] ★★★

**Equity** means providing **all** employees with the resources and support they need to succeed. [53]

Sometimes a school will give each teacher *the same* resources and time and expect everyone to succeed. But teachers will all have different requirements to fulfil their role, and the demands upon them can change year on year. An **equal** approach will work for some teachers but not for others, while an **equity** approach works for everybody.

This is recognised in the workload agreements, where Principals are instructed to provide **individualised** DTBs, considering the individual responsibilities of each teacher. [13,28,] ★★★

The use of generic time budgets is unlikely to fulfil the requirement for an individualised DTB, and it is also advised against by the NAHT (headteachers' union), who are experts in issues affecting school leaders. [54]

The best mechanism to ensure equity in workload distribution is by facilitating open, evidence-based, dialogue between teachers and Principals when planning DTBs.

## Open evenings and PTCs

Attendance at open evenings and Parent Teacher conferences is **directed time** and must come out of a teacher's Directed Time budget. [6,9] ★★★

These events should be on the **school calendar**, **issued before** the start of the academic year. [24] ★★★

If an open evening or PTC takes place in the evening after normal school hours, consideration should be given to "**trapped time**" and travel costs. [29] ★★★

For example, if students leave at 3.30pm and staff are expected to be on site to prepare for an open evening at 4pm, this is "trapped time" and must be included in teachers' directed time budget.

If, however, staff are not required to be back in school until 5.30pm, they have time to go home before the event, and it is therefore **not** trapped time.

However, staff are **entitled to claim** for travel costs if they must travel to and from school for a second time during a single day.

Many schools do PTCs during school hours, which will be "time budget neutral" as it takes place during previously allocated Directed Time.

# Twilights

"Twilights" are sessions in the **afternoon** and **early evening** where teacher remain on school premises to carry out Directed Time tasks.

They are typically used to allow teachers to "bank" hours against another day to extend a period of holiday or finish the last day of term early.

There is nothing in the TNCs which specifically talks about twilights, but TNC 2024/2 mentions the need for consultation, agreement and notice for working unsocial hours. [9]★★★

Most schools **consult** with teachers and union representatives before putting twilights into a diary.

The NAHT (headteachers' union) recommend that Principals do not use twilights for a variety of reasons.[54]★★

When planning a twilight session Principals will still be bound by relevant legislation, such as equality law and Health and Safety law.

This is a complex area as many teachers like twilights if they gain a day elsewhere in the year, so it is a matter for consultation between teachers, leaders and unions. If a twilight is causing issues where you work, consult your union for advice.

# The Annual Calendar

The school calendar is one of the most important documents produced by school leaders each year.

**All** the **activities** taking place in the school should be on the **annual calendar**, including **meetings** and **training** events throughout the year. This **must** be issued prior to start of the academic year. [24]★★★

Teachers plan their year around the school calendar, so **significant changes** *during* the school year to when events happen, can mean that some staff **cannot attend** because they made plans based on the old dates. Teachers **do not** have to give details about these prior commitments, just that they have already made plans based on the previous calendar.

Changing *which* events happen during scheduled sessions during the year is reasonable, but sufficient notice should be given to teachers so they can plan accordingly.

Teachers **cannot** be directed for **more than 195 days** each year, of which **no more than 190 days** can involve teaching students. Directing teachers to take part in any event, however brief, **counts** as one of the 195 days. [3,10,54]★★★ This includes religious events. However, if a teacher **volunteers** for an activity, it **does not** count toward the 195 days.

## In Year Variation

Sometimes changes occur during the year which are outside of anyone's control. In such cases the role and responsibilities of individual teachers may change, along with their timetable and calendar.

This should always be done with consultation with the staff members concerned so all parties can agree on what the redeployment will entail. In effect, the redeployment requires the Principal to redistribute that teacher's Directed Time. [11,12] ★★★

**Unless** a teacher moves from a classroom teacher contract onto a VP or Principal contract (see p44), the workload agreements described in this book still apply after redeployment. As usual, communication is key for in year variation to work.

## "Gained Time"

When examination classes go on study leave in England their timetabled time is known as "gained time", where teachers are now "free" to do other work. No such formal arrangement currently exists in NI.

This is a complex and often debated issue, so if a teacher finds themselves being directed to use such time for other tasks they should talk to their union for advice.

# An Inspector calls

The call from the Education and Training Inspectorate (ETI) often heralds extensive additional workload as the school prepares materials they believe ETI will want to see during their inspection visit. Additionally, the expectation of an imminent ETI inspection can be used by managers to justify excessive workload.

This should never happen.

Since the advent of the new inspection framework, ETI have been clear in stating categorically that teachers and schools should not be preparing documentation relating to inspection. [57]★★★

This is important as ETI want to inspect objectively and fairly on the everyday quality of provision, so that the needs of an organisation can be accurately identified and supported. [42]★★★

Ideally, the things ETI want to see should already be happening as part of the directions in staff time budgets, so no additional workload should be required if that phone starts to ring.

# Thinking time is working time

In August 2011 the ETI published a document called "The Reflective Teacher", which provided an excellent framework for that most important of teacher soft skills: the ability to self-reflect.

This aimed to build a culture whereby teachers were continually challenging themselves to improve by a process of organised self-reflection. By doing so ETI clearly identified structured thinking time as a core competency for a successful teaching career.

Thinking time is not specifically mentioned in either the teaching contract or the TNC documents, however it is alluded to as part of individual and collaborative PPA. [46]

While nobody is arguing that teachers should be given a few hours each week to "reflect", in too many establishments "working" is equated with "being seen to be working". Unless a teacher is tapping furiously on a keyboard or scribbling on piles of books, they are not *working*.

This is simply false. Workload should include providing teachers with the space to reflect, imagine, innovate and improve, so that they can deliver the best possible experiences to learners.

Ten minutes of quiet reflection might be the most effective use of a teachers' time on any given day.

# Part-time teachers

**All** the rules and guidelines about workload apply to part-time teachers.

Part-time teachers work a "Full-time equivalent" contract (**FTE**), which is used to calculate their *pro rata* obligations under the Jordanstown Agreement.

For example, a teacher on a 0.8 FTE contract will be contracted to work for 1265 x 0.8 hours, giving them 1012 hours of directed time each year.

Part-time teachers usually have **dedicated days** on which they work, and they **cannot** be directed to work on days **outside** of their working days without consultation, agreement and sufficient notice.

Additionally, if a part-time teacher agrees to work on a day they don't normally work on, they **must** receive that **time back** *in lieu* or via an additional payment.

As with other teachers, if a part-time teacher **volunteers** for **extracurricular activities**, it **does not** count toward directed time or their *pro rata* days.

Part-time DTBs can be complex, so teachers should carefully check their hours and days of work. If their DTB doesn't make sense they should speak to their line manager, and if they are still concerned that they are working too many hours they should contact their union for further advice.

# NISTR (sub) teachers

Almost one-third of teachers in Northern Ireland are substitute teachers, mainly through the NISTR register. There are four main types of substitute teacher, their use governed by strict rules[56]★★★:

- Long-term supply employed on fixed-term full-time contracts by a school to cover within that school.

- Long-term supply teachers on NISTR, paid on a daily rate, with no contract, notice-period or security.

- Short-term supply teachers on NISTR, as above.

- Daily supply teachers, working on an *ad hoc* basis.

Teachers' workload agreements apply to substitute teachers too, including the right to a DTB. However, many sub teachers do not receive these rights.

Many substitute teachers understandably see a short-medium term sub position as a "foot in the door" to a more permanent contract, therefore few are willing to "rock the boat" when tasked with unfair or unreasonable workloads.

This is complex, so to do justice for substitute colleagues we have asked an expert to write about these issues on our website, which we will promote on our usual channels once live. Regardless, NISTR teachers should seek professional union support if they have workload issues needing addressed.

# Early Career Teachers

Teaching sits in a peculiar space between career and vocation, and that can be a dangerous place for an idealistic teacher to be. So here is some food for thought for our ECT colleagues.

One. You are an employee, not a pupil. The Principal is not your headteacher; they are your colleague. School is your workplace, not your *alma mater*. Establish professional relationships from the outset.

Two. Teaching is an important job, but there are many other important jobs too. (E.g. medic, police officer, firefighter, *etc*). All of these jobs are compensated for overtime, but teaching is not.

Three. Workload management agreements exist to help teachers remain healthy and able to do their job successfully. [22]★★★ If you ignore these rules you put your health and career at risk.

Four. You may have been told that "going the extra mile" might advance your career. But with a third of teachers leaving within five years, not managing workload can end your career just as easily [25].

Five. You cannot pour from an empty cup. The time outside of your 1265 hours of work is when you grow and flourish as an individual, and it's through building richness in the "life" part of the work/life balance that you sustain a rich "work" part in turn.

# VPs and Principals

School leaders are employed under a different contract to classroom teachers, found in Schedule 1 and Schedule 2 of the Jordanstown Agreement.

Outside of the Working Time directive, VPs and Principals have **no contractual limit** to their working hours.

However, teaching Vice-Principals **are** subject to the weekly limits of teaching time. [20]★★★:

Teaching Principals are provided with two "release days" per week to focus on their leadership tasks, which was reinforced as part of the 2025 pay deal.

While the think1265 campaign is focused on the classroom teachers, it would be remiss of us not to mention the workload crisis facing school leaders.

Almost a third of school leaders appointed under the age of 50 leave their post within five years, more than half of whom go on to quit teaching entirely.

Principals may have been successful in applying for a leadership position, but they weren't granted superpowers. They are human beings, and need a reasonable, healthy and achievable working life too.

It is difficult to see how a school can succeed with exhausted leaders, so workload management for VPs and Principals must be a priority too.

# Identifying workload issues

These simple questions can help decide if a teacher has a workload issue which needs to be addressed.

*Do you regularly have to prepare and mark lessons outside of school hours?*

*Do you often feel unprepared for lessons each day?*

*Do you have to bring work other than preparing or marking lessons home with you?*

*Do you have to work at weekends or during holidays to keep up with your workload?*

*Do you come into work early, or stay later after work, to keep up to date with your workload?*

*Is your dedicated PPA each week interrupted or eroded by other, more pressing, demands?*

If a teacher answers "yes" to one or more of these questions, it is possible that their workload is not being properly managed. This can be because of demands from managers, or because the teacher is placing too many demands upon themselves.

Regardless of the reason, the starting point to try and resolve these issues is through communication, and the best place to start is in the discussion about the Directed Time budget.

# Discussing the DTB

Principals are asked to **seek to agree** the contents of each teacher's DTB. [12]★★★ This can be through a meeting with the Principal themselves, or a meeting with the Principal's representative.

In some schools a Principal will distribute a DTB and offer to meet with staff *should they have queries about it*. There are many reasons why this is not best practice.

In contrast, by ensuring that they or their deputies meet with staff each year, school leaders build a better understanding of the **demands** upon their teachers. This gives them the information they need to **best deploy** staff to achieve their aims for their school, which is one of their core functions. [11]★★★

If a teacher's DTB is not right they could exhaust their hours during the year, [13]★★★ effectively leaving the Principal short a staff member for a particular task. Teachers might also pursue a grievance against the Principal about their DTB, which could result in an industrial dispute in the school. [36]★★★

Therefore, it is in the interests of all stakeholders to ensure that DTBs are fit for purpose, helping to avoid issues down the line.

# Make discussions constructive

The aim of the DTB meeting is to **agree** the range of **tasks** and **time** allocated to each teacher.

Our online form can identify issues with DTBs. Trade Unions also have excellent checklists teachers can use. These help to frame issues which need raised in the DTB discussion.

DTBs are lists of tasks for the year ahead, so they should be **easy** to **understand**. Each task should have **sufficient time** allocated to it, and it should be **clear** when in the year these things will happen. Remember the **3Ts**, and **CRAM**. (p.10)

If this is not the case, then the DTB discussion is an opportunity to clarify these issues with the Principal and seek an **agreed outcome**. It is useful to follow up this meeting with an email, **confirming** what was agreed.

By taking a **flexible** and **collaborative** approach in this meeting, good Principals can build positive relationships with staff while also ensuring they can discharge their roles within contractual hours.

In contrast, a few teachers told us that they had been threatened with disciplinary action if they did not sign their DTBs last year. There is no obligation to do this, and if this happens a teacher should formally pause the meeting and contact their union.

# When things go wrong

However hard we try, things sometimes go wrong.

We have written extensively on our site about what to do when this happens, linked here.

We cannot overemphasise how important it is that teachers **seek help** from their **union** when they experience difficulties with their DTB and workload.

Teachers can **individually** or **collectively** raise workload concerns and can **ask their union** to **act** on their **behalf**. Teachers don't have to stick their head above the parapet on their own. [36]★★★

Some issues are easily fixed, while others lead to complex disputes. In such cases the **expertise** and **legal resources** of your **union** prove invaluable.

# What should a teacher do?

If you have a **workload** issue, the best thing you can do is to **record** *everything* about what's happening in a way you can access **at home**. Forward relevant emails to your personal address, and record information using your own devices or notebook. Make a note of meetings and conversations, including date, time, who was there, and what was said. **Do not** use C2K systems for this.

(Note: do not send sensitive information about learners or confidential school business to your personal accounts or devices, as you could be breaching school policies by doing so.)

When you have gathered this information, you should speak to your school union representative or contact your union directly.

Explain what your concerns are, what you have already tried to do about it, and what the evidence is to support your concerns. Your union or union rep can then work with you to resolve them.

If other teachers are experiencing similar problems, then several teachers can **come together** to address these. These can then be managed **collectively** by your union, often without naming individuals, but your union can advise further about this.

This Wee Little Book is **not** a substitute for the help of your union, **nor** is it a dispute playbook. It simply outlines what teachers' terms and conditions say about workload, linked to the relevant legislation and guidance.

But by knowing how things **should** be working, we can spot when they're **not working**.

And together we can do something about it.

Education, as always, creates change.

# Skynet isn't coming to save you

Large Language Models (LLMs, known as "AI") are being hailed as a potential solution to reduce workload, but there are reasons to be cautious.

Firstly, a teacher is **responsible** for **any resource** they use which has been **generated** using **LLMs**. [55]★★★ So, while producing a podcast from a set of notes takes moments, teachers must listen to every word carefully, checking for accuracy, and making sure the LLM doesn't channel the far right.[58]

Checking resources is nothing new, but this would extend to many other things, such as emails, risk assessments, reports, results analysis, *etc*. While good prompts help, LLMs still regularly make errors – sometimes significant ones. Furthermore, LLMs are increasingly training themselves on the output of other LLMs, which compounds these errors.

Secondly, we should be watchful to ensure that managers don't **reduce the time** teachers have for existing tasks by citing **LLM tools**. Perhaps proper AI will one day do this work in a reliable and safe way, but in the meantime teachers still need time on their time budget. AI is not a magic wand for workload, and it can't put the lid back on the Pritt stick.

At least not yet.

# Keeping Healthy

A little mild stress, now and then, is good for you. Occasional challenges are stimulating, forcing us to raise our performance, while overcoming them can be rewarding and affirming. Life would be dull if we didn't face some challenge now and then.

Yet facing challenges more frequently, particularly insurmountable challenges, creates a different kind of stress entirely. This negative stress is unhealthy and debilitating, lowering our performance. In turn this poorer performance generates even more negative stress. [59]★★

Unreasonable workload on a regular basis is a perfect recipe for creating this kind of negative stress, causing physical, emotional and behavioural symptoms in the sufferer. [60]★★★

It is important that educators can spot the warning signs of this type of stress, not only in ourselves, but in those around us too.

The common theme running through these symptoms is **change** from how a person normally is.

**Physical** symptoms range from feeling tired or exhausted much of the time; to disrupted sleep patterns and headaches. People get ill more often, experiencing physical symptoms which range from joint pain and neuralgia, to nausea and palpitations.

**Emotionally**, sufferers can feel helpless or trapped, overwhelmed and demotivated. Their sense of joy is lessened, and they can become detached and distant from those around them.

Together these symptoms cause significant **behavioural changes** in the workplace, with a reduction in performance and higher than normal absenteeism. Sufferers can become isolated from colleagues, short-tempered and easily frustrated, experiencing limited resilience and frequently self-medicating.

**All** of these behaviours are markers of **burnout**, which is a serious WHO-recognised syndrome.[61] While external factors can exacerbate burnout, it is – by definition – caused by **chronic workplace stress**.

If you recognise these symptoms you should go and **speak to your GP** as a matter of **urgency**. The earlier this condition is addressed, the faster and more complete will be the recovery. So don't ignore these symptoms, or "push through" to the next break.

The TNC agreements mentioned in this book are designed to keep teachers safe from harmful levels of stress, while helping them deliver the top-class teaching and learning our students deserve. But unless all of us – from teachers to managers – ensure they are finally implemented, we will continue to lose educators to **avoidable** stress and burnout.

# Afterword

Well, you made it! Our congratulations to those who made it through to this final part of the book.

So why is this stuff important? Why have two random teachers spent 16 months shouting about it?

Each of us, if we're lucky, get about one thousand months on this planet, and we have to squeeze our whole lives into that time.

And we deserve those months to be rich and rewarding. A life well lived.

Work is an important part of building that richness, particularly work as transformative as teaching. But our lives outside of work are important too.

At its most basic level, work is a transactional arrangement, where a person trades a portion of their life in return for a salary.

In essence, we trade our heartbeats for money. For a new teacher that's around 170 heartbeats per £1 of salary they earn.

So, why is this stuff important?

For each of us there comes a day with no tomorrow, when those heartbeats finally run out.

And when that day comes, not one of us will wish we'd spent more of our free time marking.

# References

1. TNC 2024/2 section 3.1: *"Directed Time means time spent on any activity which the Principal has determined that Teacher shall undertake. A Teacher shall be available to perform such duties at such times and such places as may reasonably be specified by the Principal. All the time that a Teacher has to be on school premises is included in Directed Time. Time spent off school premises in preparing and marking lessons is not included in a Teacher's Directed Time."*

2. TNC 2024/2 section 1.2.2.iii: *"Teachers are required to have a break of a minimum of 30 minutes between 12 noon and 2pm and are entitled to leave their place of work during this time."*

3. TEACHERS' (TERMS AND CONDITIONS OF EMPLOYMENT) REGULATIONS (NORTHERN IRELAND) 1987, Schedule 3, para 4, section a: *"A full-time Teacher, other than a Teacher employed in a residential establishment, shall be* ***available for work on 195 days in any year****, of which not more than 190 days should involve teaching children in a classroom situation."*

4. TEACHERS' (TERMS AND CONDITIONS OF EMPLOYMENT) REGULATIONS (NORTHERN IRELAND) 1987, Schedule 3, para 4, section b: *"A Teacher, other than a Teacher employed in a residential establishment, shall be available to perform such duties at such times and such places as may reasonably be specified by the Principal, or where he is employed by an Employing Authority on terms under which he is not assigned to any one school by the Employing Authority or the Principal of any school in which he may be for the time being be required to work as a Teacher,* ***for 1265 hours in any year*** *exclusive of time spent off school premises in preparing and marking lessons and time spent travelling to and from the place of work." (Bold added)*

5. TEACHERS' (TERMS AND CONDITIONS OF EMPLOYMENT) REGULATIONS (NORTHERN IRELAND) 1987, Schedule 3, para 4, section g: *"For the purposes of this paragraph a 'year' means a period of 12*

*months commencing on 31st July and a 'week' means a period of 7 days commencing on a Sunday."*

6. TNC 2024/2 section 5.1 e: *"There is a range of other professional activities that go on regularly within schools. If a Teacher is expected to carry out any duty that is deemed reasonable and in balance with the duties allocated to colleagues, then it must also be accounted for in the time budget. Due attention must be paid to ensure that there is work/life balance, in line with the Strategy for Teacher Health and Wellbeing in Northern Ireland (TNC 2011/1), particularly where a Teacher volunteers to take on additional duties on an unremunerated basis."*

7. TNC 2025/1 paragraph 14: *"These agreements outline the maximum teaching hours per week, working days per year, and that full-time teachers will spend 1265 hours per year on activities determined by the Principal (known as "directed time"). They also acknowledge that additional time needed to prepare and mark lessons is not included in directed time and to that extent is a matter of professional judgement for teachers in meeting the needs of their role. TNC 2024/2 meanwhile outlines that a portion of directed time (10%) is allowed for planning, preparation, and assessment (PPA)."*

8. Working Time Regulations (Northern Ireland) 2016 part II Regulation 4: *"(1) Unless an employer has first obtained the worker's agreement in writing to perform such work, a worker's working time, including overtime, in any reference period which is applicable in the case of that worker, shall not exceed an average of 48 hours for each seven days.*

*(2) An employer shall take all reasonable steps, in keeping with the need to protect the health and safety of workers, to ensure that the limit specified in paragraph (1) is complied with in the case of each worker employed, by the employer, in relation to whom it applies and shall keep up-to-date records of all workers who carry out work to which it does not apply by reason of the fact that the employer has obtained the worker's agreement as mentioned in paragraph (1).."* (NB: the 48 hour limit is based on average hours over 17 weeks.)

9. TNC 2024/2 section 1.2.2.ii: *"That workloads will be such that contractual duties will normally be completed within contractual hours. Actual work patterns may vary to meet the needs of the school, the department and, if appropriate, the individual but will not involve regular directed working during unsocial hours except with consultation and agreement and with a minimum of 5 working days' notice."*

10. TNC 2024/2 section 5.2: *"A Teacher's directed time of 1,265 hours per year is the basic legal requirement for a Teacher to satisfy his/her contractual obligations. A Teacher cannot be directed to undertake duties beyond 1,265 hours on 195 days. However, schools have always been dependent on a commitment from Teachers beyond the legal minimum requirement and this guidance does not change this. Schools would, for example, find it impossible to include within a Teacher's 1,265 hours all of the time currently given by Teachers to such activities as games, drama, music and school trips. Nevertheless, the extent of this commitment is for each Teacher to determine for himself or herself. Teachers should be given reasonable notice before being directed to undertake evening duties. If a Teacher agrees to carry out these duties on a voluntary basis they will not count as directed time, however, if the duties are directed by the Principal then the hours fall under directed time."*

11. TEACHERS' (TERMS AND CONDITIONS OF EMPLOYMENT) REGULATIONS (NORTHERN IRELAND) 1987, Schedule 1, para 4, section 3a: (The Professional duties of a Principal shall include)*"deploying and managing all teaching and nonteaching staff of the school and allocating particular duties to them (including such duties of the Principal as may properly be delegated to the Vice Principal or other members of the staff), in a manner consistent with their terms and conditions of employment, maintaining a reasonable balance for each employee"*

12. TNC 2024/2 section 4.3: *"The Principal is responsible for determining a time budget to each member of the teaching staff, giving due regard to the individual responsibilities of each Teacher. The Principal should seek to agree with each Teacher the range of activities/duties which that*

*Teacher will undertake and the amount of time which that Teacher will spend on each of these. The time budget should be distributed prior to the commencement of the teaching year."*

13. EA Principal's Training on Time budgeting. Sway slide 2 (see QR code link): *"Each teacher is entitled to a Directed Time budget and it is the professional duty of principals in all schools to ensure a Directed Time budget is prepared for, and gives due regard to, the individual responsibilities of each teacher in their school. Principals and each member of staff should seek to reach agreement on a teacher's Directed Time budget; teachers do not have freedom to decide for themselves how they allocate their time. Principals should plan the use of teachers' hours carefully in conjunction with the school improvement priorities, the school calendar and the annual schedule of meetings. If they do not, there could be a danger that staff will exhaust their obligatory hours before the end of the school year."*

14. The 32.4 hours week is based on 1265 hours annually, divided by the typical 39 weeks of DT (195 days), and does not include lunchtimes.

15. TNC 2024/2 section 3.4: *"Supervision occurs when a Teacher is asked to engage in activities outside of the classroom where there is no active teaching taking place. Supervision may include tasks such as morning and afternoon breaks, wet break times, arrangements for the arrival and departure of pupils, bus supervision, school assembly, examinations etc. Where a Teacher is not required to supervise at morning or afternoon break, or where this is done on a rota basis, this period must still be defined as Directed Time. It is recognised that classroom supervision is not an effective use of a Teacher's time. However, in exceptional circumstances, a Teacher may be required to supervise, as distinct from teach, the class of an absent colleague. Unless employed under a separate contract as a mid-day supervisor, a Teacher shall not be required to undertake mid-day supervision."*

16. TNC 2024/2 section 3.6: *"Registration is Directed Time. If a Teacher is required to deliver learning or pastoral work, this period of time is considered to be teaching time in the time budget."*

17. TNC 2024/2 section 3.5: *"Attendance at School Assembly is non teaching Directed Time. Leading an assembly is considered to be teaching time in the time budget."*

18. TNC 2024/2 section 5.1a: *"It is acknowledged that the weekly limits of 23.5 hours in a secondary school and 25 hours in a primary or special school will include any time a Teacher is involved in class cover, (Section 6.3)."*

19. Guidance for Boards of Governors on THE FORMULATION AND IMPLEMENTATION OF SALARY POLICY section 4.7.2: (May 2008, updated October 2024): *"Not every task that teachers undertake outside the classroom need to be separately paid for through the allocation of a TA. Before awarding a TA, the Relevant Body must be satisfied that the duties include responsibilities that:*

- *are not required of all classroom teachers;*
- *are focused primarily on teaching and learning; and*
- *require the exercise of a teacher's professional skills and judgement.*

*Such responsibilities must also conform to at least one of the following descriptions:*

- *require the teacher(s) to lead, manage and develop a subject or curriculum area, or to lead and manage pupil development across the curriculum;*
- *have an impact on the educational progress of pupils other than the classes or groups of pupils normally assigned to the teacher(s);*
- *involve leading, developing and enhancing the teaching practice of other staff.*

20. TNC 2024/2 section 4.4.1 c: *"A Teacher may not be required to teach as distinct from supervise children in a classroom situation for more than 25 hours in any week in a primary or special school and 23.5 hours in any week in a secondary school."*

21. TEACHERS' (TERMS AND CONDITIONS OF EMPLOYMENT) REGULATIONS (NORTHERN IRELAND) 1987, Schedule 3, para 4, section c: *"A teacher may not be required to teach as distinct from supervise children in a classroom situation for more than 25 hours in any week in a primary or special school and 23.5 hours in any week in a secondary school."*

22. TNC 2024/2 section 1.1: *"The central purpose of this agreement is to enable Principals, Vice Principals and Teachers to achieve the following objectives:*

*a. to maintain and enhance the quality of teaching and learning;*

*b. to preserve, in so far as this is possible, the flexibility of the contractual framework and the professional autonomy of staff;*

*c. to ensure that members of staff are able to observe their contractual requirements, pursue their careers and undertake their day to day duties without unfair and unreasonable requirements being placed on them in relation to those duties and with sufficient time to enjoy a reasonable work/life balance;*

*d. to protect and enhance the professional relationships within a school;*

*e. to ensure that Boards of Governors as employers are aware of and in a position to meet their legal obligations with respect to employment matters and to operate within the spirit of the legislation governing Working Time and Health and Safety."*

23. HSENI (hseni.gov.uk/articles/employees, accessed 9/7/25): *"All workers have a right to work in places where risks to their health and safety are properly controlled. Health and safety is about stopping you getting hurt at work or ill through work. Your employer is responsible for*

*health and safety, but you must help. As a worker, you have a duty to take care of your own health and safety and that of others who may be affected by your actions. Health and safety legislation, therefore, requires employers and workers to cooperate."*

24. TNC 2024/2 section 5.1f: *"An annual schedule of meetings will be provided in advance of the academic year. Meetings for all staff, including those with teaching allowances will be accommodated within Directed Time budgets."*

25. SecEd, "Another year and another 40 000 teachers quit the chalkface", 11 June 2024.

26. TNC 2024/2 section 4.4.1 e & f: *"e. Subject to paragraph (f) all Teachers shall be required to have a break of at least 30 minutes between the hours of 12 noon and 2.00pm.*

*f. Teachers in nursery schools and in nursery units in primary schools shall be required to have a break of at least 30 minutes between the hours of 12 noon and 2.30pm."*

27. TNC 2024/2 section 3.2: *"Teaching occurs when a qualified Teacher delivers a lesson to pupils who are engaged in activities which contribute to their active learning. Only Teachers can carry out specified work.*

*It is acknowledged that the weekly limits of 23.5 hours in a post primary school and 25 hours in a primary or special school will include any time a Teacher is involved in class cover."*

28. "Advice on Developing Directed Time Budgets" EA, 5th June 2020, section 1.1: *"Each teacher is entitled to a Directed Time budget, and it is the professional duty of principals in all schools to ensure a Directed Time budget is prepared for, and gives due regard to, the individual responsibilities of each teacher in their school. This is not a new requirement and has been in place since 1987"*

29. DTB FAQs" EA 2022: Question 7: *"Where teaching finishes at 3:30pm and a meeting is scheduled for 4:00pm, do you include the 30 mins in between as Directed Time?"*

*Response:*

*Care should be taken when determining the start time of meetings. Time is sometimes scheduled as a comfort break between the end of the school day and the meeting. It is important to note that this "trapped" time would need to be included in the Directed Time budget."*

30. DTB FAQs EA 2022: Question 15: Response: *"Lunch breaks are unpaid and do not count towards Directed Time. Therefore, this time should not be included in the teacher's Directed Time budget. Teachers in nursery schools and nursery units in primary schools are required to have a break of at least 30 minutes between the hours of 12noon and 2.30pm.*

*Setting up a classroom is not classified as teaching time. Nor is it Planning, Preparation and Assessment time. It should be included in the teacher's Directed Time budget as weekly non-teaching time, so that the teacher's overall total Directed Time doesn't exceed 1,265 hours per annum."*

31. EA Principal's Training on Time budgeting. Sway slide 8. (See reference 19, above): *"Professional communication includes activities and participation in meetings which will support: effective teaching and learning; professional collaboration; school development planning and action planning; self-evaluation processes, e.g. review and development of teaching schemes and curricular provision."*

And slide 9: *"Professional communication can take place annually as well as weekly. An example of annual communication is reporting to parents."*

32. TEACHERS' (TERMS AND CONDITIONS OF EMPLOYMENT) REGULATIONS (NORTHERN IRELAND) 1987, Schedule 3 Regulation 5, para 3: (*Non-exhaustive list of teachers' professional duties*):

*"1. Planning*

*1.1 Planning and preparing courses and lessons;*

*1.2 Teaching, according to their educational needs, the pupils assigned to him/her, including the setting and marking of work to be carried out by the pupils in school and elsewhere;*

*1.3 Assessing, recording and reporting on the development, progress and attainment of pupils.*

*2. General*

*2.1 Promoting the general progress and well-being of individual pupils and of any class or group of pupils assigned to him/her;*

*2.2 Providing advice and guidance to pupils on educational and social matters and on their further education and future careers including information about sources of more expert advice on specific questions, making relevant records and reports;*

*2.3 Making records of and reports on the personal and social needs of pupils except in instances where to do so might be regarded as compromising a teacher's own position;*

*2.4 Communicating and consulting with the parents of pupils;*

*2.5 Communicating and co-operating with such persons or bodies outside the school as may be approved by the employing authority and the Board of Governors;*

*2.6 Participating in meetings arranged for any of the purposes described above.*

*3. Assessment/Reporting*

*Providing or contributing to oral and written assessments, reports and references relating to individual pupils and groups of pupils except in instances where to do so might be regarded as compromising a teacher's own position.*

*4. Staff Development/Professional Development*

*4.1 Participating, if required, in any scheme of staff development and performance review;*

*4.2a) Reviewing from time to time his/her methods of teaching and programmes of work;*

*b) Participating in arrangements for his/her further training and professional development as a teacher.*

*4.3 Advising and co-operating with the Principal and other teachers (or any one or more of them) on the preparation and development of courses of study, teaching materials, teaching programmes, methods of teaching and assessment and pastoral arrangements.*

*5. Discipline/Health and Safety*

*5.1 Maintaining good order and discipline among pupils in accordance with the policies of the employing authority and safeguarding their health and safety both when they are authorised to be on the school premises and when they are engaged in authorised school activities elsewhere.*

*5.2 Participating in meetings at the school which relate to the curriculum for the school or the administration or organisation of the school, including pastoral arrangements.*

*6. Public Examinations*

*Participating in arrangements for preparing pupils for public examinations and in assessing pupils for the purposes of such examinations; recording and reporting such assessments; and participating in arrangements for pupils' presentation for and supervision during such examination.*

*7. Review and Development of Management Activities/Administration*

*7.1 a) Contributing to the selection for appointment and professional development of other teachers, including the induction and assessment of probationary teachers;*

*b) Co-ordinating or managing the work of other teachers;*

*c) Taking such part as may be required of him/her in the review, development and management of activities relating to the curriculum, organisation and pastoral functions of the school.*

*7.2 a) Participating in administrative and organisational tasks related to such duties as described above, including the management or supervision of persons providing support for the teachers in the school and the ordering and allocation of equipment and materials.*

*b) Subject to the provisions of Article 22 of the Order, attending assemblies;*

*c) Registering the attendance of pupils and supervising pupils, whether these duties are to be performed before, during or after school sessions."*

33. TNC2005 / 3 - PROCEDURE FOR TEACHERS WHO WORK WITH VDU AND WHO WISH TO APPLY FOR AN EYESIGHT SCREENING TEST, section 1.2: *"Teachers who operate a VDU in connection with their work for 1 hour or more per day, are eligible to apply for an eyesight screening test."* Full policy in the QR code.

34. TNC 2024/2 section 5.1d: *"Some Teachers will be in receipt of Teaching Allowances or Special Educational Needs Allowances for specific duties. These duties must also be allowed for within the time budget of 1265 hours."*

35. TNC 2025/1 Annex 1, agreed measure 2: *"Schools will be reminded to ensure their operational hours and contact methods have been communicated to parents; including that staff are not expected to respond outside of operational hours unless in a critical incident. Governors will be reminded of the Working Time Regulations and the Department and employing authorities will be mindful of these arrangements when issuing communications"*

36. TNC 2025/1 section 5.8: "*5.8.1 It is hoped that this guidance will avoid disputes in relation to Teachers' time budgets. Any Teacher who has a concern or fails to reach agreement on their time budget should raise the matter, in the first instance with the Principal. If necessary the Teacher should seek support from their recognised trade union to resolve the situation. It is hoped that such issues will be resolved without recourse to formal procedures. In circumstances, however where a Teacher is not satisfied with the outcome the appropriate grievance procedure may be used.*

*5.8.2 If the issue is impacting on a number of Teachers in the school then the Teachers and/or the Trade Union Representative (or representatives) may raise the issue with the Principal on a joint basis. Where this does not resolve the issue the Teachers may utilise the appropriate grievance procedure.*"

37. TNC 2024/2 section 3.3: "*The term 'cover' refers to any occasion where the Teacher normally responsible for teaching the class is absent and a teaching colleague is required to teach the class. Cover therefore is included within the teaching limit of 25 hours in any week in a primary school or special school and 23.5 hours in any week in a secondary school, as specified under the 1987 Regulations*"

38. TNC 2024/2 section 6.1: "*This guidance is based on provisions set out in the Teachers' (Terms and Conditions of Employment) Regulations (Northern Ireland) 1987, as amended by the Teachers' (Terms and Conditions of Employment) (Amendment) Regulations (Northern Ireland) 1988.*

*This guidance has been developed to provide a framework for Principals to ensure the provision of cover for absent Teachers is shared on a fair and equitable basis. All schools are required to develop a cover policy for the arrangements for cover during periods of Teacher absence. A model policy has been drawn up to assist schools (see*

*Section 7). Any significant variation to or review of the model policy will take place following consultation with the recognised trade unions. The policy should be known and available to all staff, detail the normal arrangements whereby classes will be covered and how this will be achieved. The policy should cover arrangements for planned and unplanned absence. It is recommended that the implementation of cover arrangements is monitored by the Principal, on a regular basis, in consultation with the recognised trade unions' representatives in the school, to ensure that a fair and equitable distribution of cover duties amongst teaching staff is achieved. The ICT management systems in schools may assist with this process."*

39. TNC 2024/2 section 6.2.2: *"In addition, the professional duties of a Principal include:*

*'ensuring that the duty of providing cover for absent teachers, as set out in paragraph (9) of Schedule 3 is shared equitably among all teachers in the school, taking account of their teaching and other duties" and "participating, to such extent as may be appropriate having regard to his other duties, in the teaching of the pupils at the school, including the provision of cover for absent teachers'."*

40. TEACHERS' (TERMS AND CONDITIONS OF EMPLOYMENT) REGULATIONS (NORTHERN IRELAND) 1987, Schedule 3, Regulation 5: *"In schools with an average daily enrolment greater than 222 pupils a teacher other than a supply teacher shall not be required to provide such cover after the second day on which a teacher, other than a teacher of primary 1 or primary 2 class or of a nursery class in a primary school, is absent or otherwise not available, or from the first day if the fact that the teacher would be absent or otherwise not available for a period exceeding 2 days was known to and agreed by the employing authority in advance."*

41. TNC 2024/2 section 6.3.3: *"It is agreed by the parties that cover arrangements are a necessary part of school life. Schools will not oblige Teachers to exceed the maximum teaching hours (23.5 in secondary schools, 25 hours in primary and special schools) in any week, taking into consideration any time allocated for management responsibilities of Teachers and for planning, preparation or assessments. Schools should*

*be cognisant of the significant workload required of Newly Qualified Teachers (NQTs) as part of their Early Professional Development (EPD). Therefore it is recommended NQTs, employed on long term or permanent contracts, should only be required to undertake cover in exceptional circumstances and this should be reflected in the School Cover Policy."*

42. ETI "New Framework for Inspection", page 2 – Purpose and Guiding Principles of Inspection.

43. TNC 2024/2 section 7.6: *"A system which is transparent and fair will be put in place to record and monitor the allocation of cover to ensure this does not exceed Teachers' contractual obligations. The allocation of cover duties to each Teacher will be reviewed on a regular basis to ensure fair and equitable distribution of cover duties amongst Teachers is achieved and maintained. In the event that a Teacher is found to have undertaken more cover than the recommended, this will be offset against any future cover allocation to this Teacher to ensure the maximum teaching hours are not exceeded. The Principal/SMT (amend as appropriate) will carry out an annual review of the cover policy in consultation with the recognised trade unions' representatives in the school and will update the policy when required."*

44. TNC 2024/2 section 5.3: *"Principals cannot direct Teachers to take pupils on educational visits involving overnight stays. Where this takes place on a voluntary basis it is a matter of negotiation between the Teacher and the Principal as to the amount of directed time which will be allocated to this activity out of the annual time budget. This should include an appropriate allocation of time for the organisation of such visits."*

45. TNC 2024/2 section 1.2.1: *"Parties to this agreement accept and acknowledge that teaching staff have the right to:*

*i. reasonable workloads;*

*ii. a fair distribution of work within the school and to raise concerns where this is not the case;*

*iii. carry out their duties within socially acceptable working hours;*

*iv. regular daily, weekly and annual breaks from work;*

*v. enjoy other rights as specified in contractual terms and conditions and in other agreements without pressure to rescind or restrict these rights other than on a temporary basis and where there has been consultation and agreement.*

*1.2.2 Arising from the principles above and fundamental to this agreement, are four entitlements applying to all Teachers:*

*i. That workloads will continue to be managed in an open, fair and equitable way at departmental/school level and that Teachers are able to challenge unfair and/or unreasonable distribution of workload.*

*ii. That workloads will be such that contractual duties will normally be completed within contractual hours. Actual work patterns may vary to meet the needs of the school, the department and, if appropriate, the individual but will not involve regular directed working during unsocial hours except with consultation and agreement and with a minimum of 5 working days' notice.*

*iii. Teachers are required to have a break of a minimum of 30 minutes between 12 noon and 2pm and are entitled to leave their place of work during this time.*

*iv. Where a Teacher and his or her line manager fail to reach agreement on any of the above, in the first instance the Teacher should raise the matter informally and may refer the matter to the Board of Governors using the appropriate grievance procedure."*

46. TNC 2024/2 section 5.6: *"The intended purpose of planning, preparation and assessment (PPA) time is to enable Teachers to raise standards through individual or collaborative professional activity and improve Teachers' work/life balance. PPA time has the potential to impact positively on the twin aims of raising standards and tackling Teacher workload. The practice of Teachers carrying out their planning,*

*preparation and assessment outside of their normal teaching hours, and in isolation from each other, is not considered satisfactory by the Teachers' Negotiating Committee. In 2020 the Teachers' Negotiating Committee agreed that 10% of Teachers' Directed Time budget will be allowed for Planning, Preparation and Assessment (PPA)."*

47. DTB FAQs EA 2022: Question 3: *"Should a senior member of staff on, say a 30% teaching timetable, who has additional management time built in, still be awarded the full 126.5hrs of PPA or should it be 30% of this?*

*Response:*

*10% of every teacher's time budget must be ring-fenced for planning, preparation, and assessment time. For a full-time teacher, that is 126.5 hours per annum. Any member of staff who has additional responsibilities should have these reflected in their time budget in addition to their PPA time. In this example, the teacher is teaching for 30% of their 1,265 hours. A further 10% should be allocated to PPA. The remaining 60% is allocated to other duties, some of which will be in relation to his / her role as a senior teacher."*

48. TNC 2020/1 section 6, bullet 2: *"10% of teachers' Directed Time budget will be allowed for Planning, Preparation and Assessment (PPA)."*

49. Advice on Developing Directed Time Budgets (EA) June 2020, section 4.4.5: *"The Pay & Workload Agreement, April 2020, guarantees that 10% of a teacher's Directed Time (i.e. 126½ hours per annum) is set aside for Planning, Preparation and Assessment. (PPA). This dedicated PPA time will enable a teacher to raise standards through individual and collaborative professional activity. The Teachers' (Terms and Conditions of Employment) Regulations (Northern Ireland) 1987, in regard to working time, states that a teacher shall be available to perform such duties at such times and such places as may reasonably be specified by the Principal. School managements should ensure that a teacher's PPA time is not eroded by demands and should be kept available for teachers to individually prepare, work, plan, mark and meet collaboratively with their colleagues."*

50. TNC 2025/1 Heads of Agreement point 26. *"Management Side, further to engagement with NITC, will jointly engage with practitioners and officials to consider the workload associated with, and effectiveness of approaches to, short, medium & long-term planning; as well as evaluation through pupil observation in Early Years & Special Schools."*

51. Private correspondence with HSENI, June 2025: *"The working time regulations would normally apply to additional work at home unless the employment contract includes on opt out clause. The employer can set expected hours for prepping lessons etc. If the amount of time spent at home prepping lessons and marking work etc. is seen as excessive by a teacher, they should bring this to their managers attention."*

52. Guidance for Boards of Governors on THE FORMULATION AND IMPLEMENTATION OF SALARY POLICY section 4.7.2: (May 2008, updated October 2024): *"Not every task that teachers undertake outside the classroom need to be separately paid for through the allocation of a TA. Before awarding a TA, the Relevant Body must be satisfied that the duties include responsibilities that:*

- *are not required of all classroom teachers;*
- *are focused primarily on teaching and learning; and*
- *require the exercise of a teacher's professional skills and judgement.*

*Such responsibilities must also conform to at least one of the following descriptions:*

- *require the teacher(s) to lead, manage and develop a subject or curriculum area, or to lead and manage pupil development across the curriculum;*
- *have an impact on the educational progress of pupils other than the classes or groups of pupils normally assigned to the teacher(s);*
- *involve leading, developing and enhancing the teaching practice of other staff.*

53. *What does it mean to be equitable?* [online] The HR Lady LLC. Available at: https://thehrlady.com/what-does-it-mean-to-be-equitable/ [Accessed 23 Jul. 2025].

*"For example, in employment, being equitable means providing all employees with the resources and support they need to succeed rather than just providing these resources to some employees while denying them to others."*

54. Glenister, S. (2023). NAHT(NI) guidance on producing a time budget with exemplars for each sector. [online] NAHT. [Accessed 23 Jul. 2025].

55. Department for Education (2025). *Generative Artificial Intelligence (AI) in Education*. [online] GOV.UK.

Available at: https://www.gov.uk/government/publications/generative-artificial-intelligence-in-education/generative-artificial-intelligence-ai-in-education.

"Generative Artificial Intelligence in Education": *"Teachers, leaders and staff must use their professional judgement when using these tools. Any content produced requires critical judgement to check for appropriateness and accuracy. The quality and content of any final documents remains the responsibility of the professional who produced it and the organisation they belong to, regardless of the tools or resources used."*

56. See TNC 2016/1, THE APPROPRIATE USE OF THE NORTHERN IRELAND SUBSTITUTE TEACHER REGISTER (NISTR) AND ENGAGEMENT OF SUBSTITUTE TEACHERS IN ALL SCHOOLS

57. Private communication between authors and ETI, June 2025

58. Taylor, J. (2025). Musk's AI firm forced to delete posts praising Hitler from Grok chatbot. [online] the Guardian.

59. Sapolsky, R.M. (2017). Behave: the biology of humans at our best and worst. London: Bodley Head, pp.127–131.

60. Mental Health UK (2024). Burnout. [online] Mental Health UK. Available at: https://mentalhealth-uk.org/burnout/. [Accessed 23 Jul. 2025]

61. World Health Organization (2019). Burn-out an 'occupational phenomenon': International classification of diseases. [online] World Health Organization. Available at: https://www.who.int/news/item/28-05-2019-burn-out-an-occupational-phenomenon-international-classification-of-diseases.[Accessed 23 Jul. 2025]

For help and advice about workplace stress and burnout, scan the QR code below:

# What's next?

The 2025-26 academic year will be a key year for the management of workload in Northern Ireland's schools.

In April 2025 the Management Side announced a wide range of time-bound workload-related actions, over the next 12 months Readers can read this document through the QR link below:

The Minister's Independent Review of Workload panel is due to report in November 2025, and they are expected to make an additional set of recommendations about managing workload.

While together these issues should help to improve the situation regarding workload, it is vital to remember that TNC 2024/2 **is still** in force and has been since August 2024.

The guidelines in this book are based on this agreement, and it remains up to teachers everywhere – in association with their respective unions – to ensure that these agreements are being implemented in their schools.

Unless existing agreements, and those which are about to be made, are finally implemented in schools, the workload crisis will never be fully resolved.

# The Workload Vicious Cycle

The graphic below shows how a failure to implement the workload agreements outlined in this book leads to industrial dispute in education.

Perhaps this year is the year that teachers, leaders and employers finally short-circuit this destructive cycle once and for all.

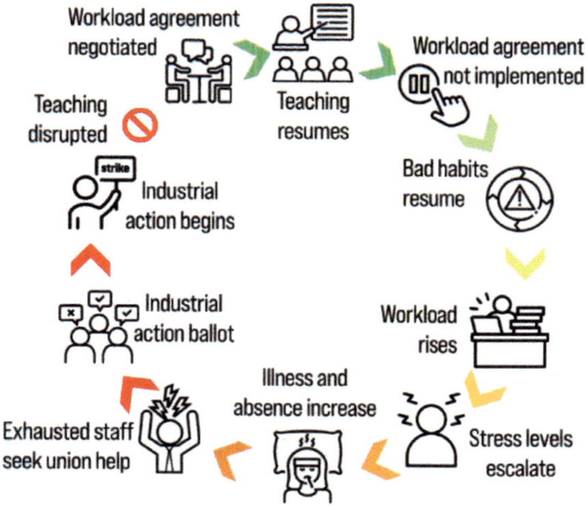